D0753306

Raccoons

by **Steven Otfinoski**

mc **Marshall Cavendish**
Benchmark
New York

Thanks to Larry Battson, Wildlife Educational Services, Inc., for his expert reading of this manuscript.

Other Marshall Cavendish Offices:
Marshall Cavendish International (Asia) Private Limited, 1 New Industrial Road, Singapore 536196 • Marshall Cavendish International (Thailand) Co Ltd. 253 Asoke, 12th Flr, Sukhumvit 21 Road, Klongtoey Nua, Wattana, Bangkok 10110, Thailand • Marshall Cavendish (Malaysia) Sdn Bhd, Times Subang, Lot 46, Subang Hi-Tech Industrial Park, Batu Tiga, 40000 Shah Alam, Selangor Darul Ehsan, Malaysia

Marshall Cavendish is a trademark of Times Publishing Limited

All websites were available and accurate when this book was sent to press.

Library of Congress Cataloging-in-Publication Data
Otfinoski, Steven.
Raccoons / by Steven Otfinoski.
p. cm. — (Animals animals)
Includes index.
Summary: "Provides comprehensive information on the anatomy, special skills, habitats, and diet of raccoons"—Provided by publisher.
ISBN 978-0-7614-4841-9
1. Raccoon—Juvenile literature. I. Title.
QL737.C26O84 2011
599.76'32—dc22
2009022630

Photo research by Joan Meisel

Cover photo: Jacob Taposchaner/Getty Images

The photographs in this book are used by permission and through the courtesy of:
Alamy: tbkmedia.de, 1, 8, 23; Arco Images Gmbh, 4, 14; Forest Light, 16; David Hosking, 13; Top-Pics TBK, 19; John Pickles, 22; Gary Crabbe, 32. *Getty Images*: Joe Drivas, 6; Steve Maslowski, 11; Joe McDonald, 18; Joseph Van Os, 20, 29; Daniel J. Cox, 24; Jim Simmen, 26; Taylor S Kennedy, 28; AFP, 31, 35; James Kroemer, 36. *Peter Arnold, Inc.*: Usher, D., 37.

Editor: Joy Bean
Publisher: Michelle Bisson
Art Director: Anahid Hamparian
Series Designer: Adam Mietlowski

Printed in Malaysia (T)
135642

Contents

Masked Mischief Maker

A father and mother and their two children were quietly watching television one evening in their home in New York City when they heard animal noises coming from the kitchen. The father went to investigate. He found a raccoon eating out of their cat's food bowl in the kitchen. The raccoon scurried to the basement and ran out the small cat entrance at the bottom of the door. The father closed tight the metal door over the cat entrance to prevent the raccoon from returning. Then he went back to watching television with his family.

A short time later, the family again heard noises in the kitchen. The father ran in and was surprised to see the same raccoon devouring the cat's food. When

Raccoons are able to use the toes on their paws to reach for things, grab at things, and lift things.

he chased the animal again, it lifted the metal door with its forepaw and scooted out. "I have to have a certain amount of respect for them," the father later told a news reporter. "They [raccoons] have managed to survive in this tough city like the rest of us."

Raccoons are among the craftiest of animals. They can use the long toes of their forepaws like human fingers to lift open a pet door, unscrew a jar, or remove the

Raccoons are easily recognizable by the black band of fur surrounding their eyes.

closed lid on a garbage can. The black band of fur that covers their eyes identifies them as clearly as the stripes on the back of a skunk. Their face mask announces to the world, "I am a clever fellow who knows how to slip into your house and steal your food, so watch out!" Some people think of raccoons as annoying pests. Yet many people, such as the man in New York City, come to admire them for their intelligence, their boldness, and their playfulness. The raccoon is native to the Western Hemisphere. It lives just about everywhere but northern Canada, the mountains of the western United States, and most Caribbean islands, where it was killed off by hunters centuries ago. It has been introduced successfully in parts of Europe and Asia. There are just two *species* of raccoons—the northern raccoon and the crab-eating raccoon.

The raccoon is a fur-covered *mammal* that weighs between 16 and 20 pounds (7 and 9 kilograms) and stands about 12 inches (30 centimeters) tall at the shoulder. Female raccoons are a little smaller than male ones. The other outstanding feature of the raccoon is its long, bushy tail. The tail has between four and ten black rings around it. The tail often

Did You Know . . .

The raccoon is a relative of the giant panda of China. Another relative closer to home is the coatimundi, or hog-nosed coon.

makes up to half of a raccoon's length. The raccoon's coat is mostly gray, but may have touches of yellow or brown. It has two coats of fur. The inner coat is made up of thick brown hairs that keep it warm in cold weather. The outer coat has long black and white *guard hairs*, that protect it from wind and rain, which runs off the hairs easily.

This raccoon hangs on a tree branch to rest.

Raccoons are *nocturnal* animals, which means they are active at night and sleep during the day. Their shiny black eyes reflect every gleam of light and allow them to see clearly in the dark as they hunt for food. However, they see distant objects poorly and are color-blind. Raccoons have a good sense of smell with their pointed noses. They hear the slightest sound with their 1.5-inch (3.8-cm) long ears. They have a superb sense of touch in the toes of their forepaws. Each paw, front and back, has five toes. At the end of each toe is a curved, sharp claw. These claws allow raccoons to climb trees with ease.

Species Chart

◆ The northern, or common, raccoon is 30 to 38 inches (76 to 97 cm) in length, including its tail, and weighs between 12 and 25 pounds (5 and 11 kg). It is found from southern Canada to Panama in Central America.

A Northern, or common, raccoon.

◆ The crab-eating raccoon is 16 to 20 inches (41 to 51 cm) in length and weighs between 4.4 and 26.5 pounds (2 and 12 kg). It has shorter hair and thinner underfur than the northern raccoon. It also has longer legs. It is found in the marshes and jungle regions of Central and South America and on the island republic of Trinidad and Tobago. The crab-eating raccoon is named after its favorite food. It lives near waterways where it can find crabs and other shellfish.

A crab-eating raccoon.

A Hearty Appetite

Raccoons living near humans in suburbs and cities may have a taste for pet food and garbage, but in the wild they will eat just about everything and anything. Raccoons are *omnivores*, animals that eat other animals as well as plants. Both northern raccoons and crab-eating raccoons love shellfish, not just crabs. They also eat lobsters, crayfish, and, if they live near seawater, clams and oysters. They also enjoy fish, frogs, and *tadpoles*, which are the larva, or early stage, of frogs and toads. Raccoons will eat land animals such as field mice, small snakes, snails, turtles, and birds and their eggs. In spring and summer they will also feast on acorns, seeds, nuts, berries, various

Raccoons eat a great number of things, including berries from trees and bushes.

fruits, and corn, as well as insects such as grasshoppers, crickets, and beetles. Some raccoons will even eat *carrion*, the rotting meat of dead animals.

Raccoons are very smart hunters. In fact, when they are hunting box turtles, they will look where the sun hits leaves on the forest floor. Raccoons know that in a sunny spot, there is usually a box turtle hidden there. To get them to come out of their shell, raccoons will carry the turtles in their mouths to a puddle or creek and wait for them to put their heads out underwater.

Some raccoons that live near water are able to catch fish for a meal.

The scientific name for raccoon is *Procyn lotor*, which in part is Latin for "the washer." This comes from a persistent belief among many people that raccoons wash their food before eating it. While it is true that raccoons will often dunk their food in water, most *naturalists* do not believe that raccoons are deliberately washing it. So why do they do it? There are a number of possible reasons. They may be getting rid of bad-tasting oil on the skin of a frog or toad they are about to eat. Or they may be moistening the morsel because they lack effective *salivary glands*. Or, if they are captive raccoons, they may be imitating the fishing behavior of their cousins in the wild. It is also possible that the presence of water enhances the sense of touch in the raccoons' sensitive toes and makes eating more pleasurable.

Raccoons in Canada and in the northern regions of the United States eat more food in the fall than at any other time of year. They are storing up fat in their bodies to get them through the coming winter, when there will be less food to eat. Northern raccoons crawl into their *dens*, usually hollow logs or trees,

Did You Know . . .
Raccoons will raid a beehive to get at the sweet honeycomb inside. They have little fear of the angry bees, because their thick fur protects them from the bees' stingers.

A raccoon looks to be washing its hands and food in water before eating.

and sleep for long periods during the winter. But unlike some other mammals, such as bears and skunks, they do not *hibernate*. When an animal hibernates, it goes into a very deep sleep and its body temperature and heart rate drop drastically. Raccoons do not sleep so deeply and often wake up during the winter months. They will even leave their dens on mild winter days to hunt for food or simply bask in the sun.

Raccoons are less solitary than some woodland mammals. Adult males live alone, but younger males and females will live in small, loose family groups. Each individual or small group will have a *home range* or *territory* of about 200 acres (0.8 square kilometers). Adult males may have a territory of up to 2 square miles (5.2 square km). Within this territory, they will make their dens and hunt for food. During mating season, they will venture out of their territory in search of a mate.

During the winter months, some raccoons may leave their dens to lie in the sun on a nice day.

3 Cute and Cuddly Kits

Most raccoons in northern regions will mate from January to early March. For those living farther south, mating may take place as late as June. If a male cannot find a female in its territory, it will roam outside it, traveling as far as 8 miles (13 km) in a single night. Once the male finds a mate and is accepted by her, the pair will live together in the same den for about two weeks.

At the end of the mating period, the male usually leaves, never to return. He plays no part in child rearing. The female gives birth to between one and seven babies, called *kits*, nine weeks later. An average *litter* is three to five kits. The newborns are

A pair of raccoons will live together in a single den for a few weeks as they mate.

These raccoons were just born and huddle together to stay warm.

about 4 inches (10 cm) in length and weigh only 2 ounces (57 grams). They have no black mask across their eyes and no rings on their tails. Those will appear about ten days later. The kits' ears and eyes are sealed shut. They spend the first weeks of life nursing on their mother's milk and sleeping. To keep warm, they pile on top of one another, forming a big heap. At night, while they sleep, their mother leaves the den to hunt for food. She will never be far away, however, in case a *predator* comes to eat her young. She will defend them with her life if necessary.

When the kits are about three weeks old, their ears and eyes open and their teeth start to grow in. By eight weeks they are ready to follow their mother on short hunting trips. They follow her in single file across the woodland. She shows them which plants are good to eat and how to catch a grasshopper in a meadow or a tadpole in a pond. The kits appear to

When young raccoons are old enough, their mother will take them out of the den and teach them how to look for food.

Did You Know . . .
If two male raccoons fight for the favors of a female, the female does not necessarily take the stronger of the two as a mate. She may decide she likes the loser better. The choice is up to her.

*These young raccoons,
while old enough to
leave their mother's
den, are learning that
climbing trees is not as
easy as it looks.*

like playing almost as much as eating. They will chase each other, play leapfrog, and wrestle.

By the time the kits are four months old, they are maturing into young raccoons. As fall fades and winter approaches, a few may set off to make dens of their own. But most young raccoons will spend the winter in their mother's den. By spring their mother is expecting her next litter, and her young leave to make their own dens. Some build their dens near their mother's. In captivity, raccoons can live from ten to twenty years. In the wild, they only live up to about sixteen years. But only a few fortunate ones live that long. Most have a life span of well under five years. Life for a raccoon in the wild is full of dangers.

4 Predators and Disease

Raccoons are threatened by a number of predators in nature. They include coyotes, foxes, wolves, bobcats, and cougars. Predatory birds such as great horned owls and hawks also attack and eat raccoons. Because raccoons are active at night, they go unseen by some predators who hunt by day.

The raccoon will fight a predator if cornered, scratching with its claws and biting with its teeth. It is a courageous fighter, but most of its predators are bigger and stronger. The raccoon's best defense, in most cases, is to flee. Usually slow and awkward on its feet, it can run as fast as 15 miles (24 km) per hour for short

The fox is one of the raccoons greatest predators.

periods. To escape an enemy, it will often climb a tree or plunge into the nearest body of water.

Raccoons are expert tree climbers. They are also excellent swimmers. Raccoons swim dog paddle–style across streams, rivers, and ponds. Most predators do not like water and will give up the chase.

Disease is as great a threat to raccoons as predators. Raccoons are vulnerable to serious illnesses such as roundworm, canine distemper, and *rabies*. Rabies

When a raccoon is being chased by a predator, it can climb a tree in order to try to get to safety.

is a fatal disease that attacks the central nervous system of mammals, including humans. It is generally spread by the bite of a rabid animal. If untreated, rabies can result in death within days.

In recent years raccoons have contacted rabies more often than any other animal in the United States. In 2004 raccoons accounted for more than a third of the 6,844 documented rabies cases. The other cases were spread mostly among skunks, bats, and foxes. There have been no documented human deaths attributed to rabid raccoons. But in the northeastern United States the number of *domestic* animals—including dogs, cats, and cattle—exposed to raccoon rabies has been on the rise.

A snarling raccoon tries to scare away a predator.

In some states and in parts of Canada, authorities treat raccoons with *vaccines* that prevent them from getting rabies. One procedure involves trapping raccoons, injecting them with the vaccine, and then releasing them. More recently, scientists have found an easier way to vaccinate. They drop the vaccine from airplanes in areas where raccoons live. The vaccine is contained in lumps of bait that are a mixture of sugar and fat. The raccoons eat the bait and consume the vaccine.

If you see a raccoon or other nocturnal wild animal acting strangely during the day, it may have rabies. Do not go near the animal but immediately call your local animal control officer. He or she will investigate and handle the animal in a safe manner.

Did You Know . . .

The raccoon is one of the few animals that can climb down a tree head first. Porcupines and other animals lack the raccoon's strong claws and agility and can only climb down backward, tail first.

In order to keep raccoons healthy, a trapper catches a raccoon so he can vaccinate the raccoon against rabies and release the animal back into the wild.

5 Raccoons and People

Raccoons and people have had a long and interesting relationship. Since the time of early Native Americans, people have told stories about raccoons and admired them for their intelligence and cleverness. But they have also hunted this same animal for its fur and meat. Native Americans traded raccoon *pelts* with European colonists for manufactured goods. The colonists and later Americans made the pelts into warm caps, overcoats, and other articles of clothing. Pioneers such as Davy Crockett were known for wearing so-called coonskin caps with the tail hanging down in the back.

Early Americans also enjoyed hunting the raccoon for its dark meat. Today, few people eat raccoon,

Raccoons are sometimes hunted for their fur. Coonskin caps are made from the skins of raccoons.

although raccoon meat remains popular in certain parts of the American South where raccoon hunting is still a sport. Hunters consider raccoon a challenge to track. The raccoon knows how to throw a hunter and his hound dogs off its scent. It will wade into a stream to wash its scent away and then return to land. It will climb a low-hanging branch of a tree and then hop back to the ground, also breaking its scent trail.

Today raccoons continue to die in large numbers. More are killed by cars while crossing roadways at night than by animal predators and hunters. Disease claims many others. In the United States, a wild raccoon's life is surprisingly brief—few of them live longer than five years. Yet the raccoon is not on any endangered species list and faces no threat of *extinction*. Why is this so? The simple answer is that there are so many of them. In the twentieth century, raccoons experienced a population explosion. They are also more adaptable to change of habitat than many other animals. When forestland is destroyed for human development, raccoons have

Did You Know . . .
President Calvin Coolidge's wife, Grace, had a pet raccoon named Rebecca. Rebecca often roamed through the White House, frightening the staff. The Coolidges eventually donated Rebecca to a zoo in Washington, D.C.

34

Animal lovers protest during a demonstration to stop department stores from carrying products that contain fur.

When raccoons' homes are destroyed by human development, raccoons then make their homes closer to humans and sometimes look for food in garbage cans.

moved into the suburbs and cities. They eat the food humans leave out in their garbage. They make their dens in barns, attics, and garages. In the last few years, the New York City Department of Parks and Recreation has reported a rise in the number of reported raccoon sightings and encounters in the city's five boroughs, or sections. Raccoons, it appears, are here to stay.

Some people like raccoons so much that they have made pets of them. Raccoons are more intelligent than cats and can be successfully trained by humans.

While keeping raccoons as pets is highly discouraged, and is illegal in some states, some people have tried to keep them as pets and train them as they would domesticated animals.

Most experts discourage people from adopting wild raccoons. It is illegal to have raccoons as pets in some states. If you want to adopt a raccoon and your state laws allow it, experts recommend getting one from a breeder. And be prepared to work hard to train it. It will take much time and patience.

Raccoons are one of the most common animals in North America. But there is nothing "common" about this fascinating and intriguing animal.

Glossary

carrion—The rotting meat of dead animals.

den—The home of an animal, often in a secluded place.

domestic—Suitable for living and working with humans.

extinction—The state of no longer existing.

guard hairs—Large, stiff outer hairs that protect the underfur of furbearing animals.

hibernate—To go into a deep sleep for the winter; something certain animals do to survive the cold and scarcity of food.

home range—The area in which an animal or plant lives.

kit—The young of raccoons or other furbearing animals.

litter—A group of young animals born at one time to a female.

mammal—A warm-blooded animal that has hair or fur and nurses its young with its own milk.

naturalist—A person who studies animals and plants.

nocturnal—Active during the night.

omnivore—An animal that eats both other animals and plants to survive.

pelts—The hides or skins of animals.

predator—An animal that preys on, or eats other animals to survive.

rabies—A fatal disease that strikes the central nervous system and is mainly spread by the bite of a rabid animal.

salivary glands—Organs in the mouth and jaw of an animal or human that secrete saliva, a fluid that aids in eating and digesting.

species—Groups of living things that share the same characteristics and mate only with their own kind.

tadpole—The larva of frogs and toads that live in water.

territory—An area that an animal lives in and defends from other animals of the same kind or species.

vaccine—A preparation of dead or weak germs that stimulates defenses in the body that prevent certain diseases.

Find Out More

Books

Hanzik, Sharon. *Raccoons Don't Use Spoons.* Denver, CO: Outskirts Press, 2009.

Landau, Elaine. *Raccoons: Scavengers of the Night* (Animals After Dark). Berkeley Heights, NJ: Enslow Publishers, 2007.

Merrick, Patrick. *Raccoons* (New Naturebook). Mankato, MN: Child's World, 2006.

Ripple, William J. *Raccoons*. Mankato, MN: Capstone Press, 2006.

Web Sites

Environmental Education for Kids (EEK!)
www.dnr.state.wi.us/org/caer/ce/eek/critter/
mammal/raccoon.htm

NatureWorks
www.nhptv.org/NatureWorks/raccoon.htm

University of Michigan Museum of Zoology
http://animaldiversity.ummz.umich.edu/site/
accounts/information/Procyon_lotor.html

The World Wide Raccoon Web
www.loomcom.com/raccoons/

Index

Page numbers for illustrations are in **boldface**.

About the Author

Steven Otfinoski is the author of numerous books about animals. He has written *Koalas, Sea Horses, Alligators, Hummingbirds, Dogs, Horses, Skunks, Pigs and Hogs,* and *Storks and Cranes* in the Animals Animals series. Otfinoski lives in Connecticut with his wife, a high school teacher and editor.